LORD, HELP US TO RECOGNIZE EACH DOOR OF...

TO PARTNER WITH HIM
TO BECOME HIS VOICE
TO REPRESENT HIM
TO CELEBRATE HIS GRACE
TO KNOW HIM

DEVERN FROMKE

Published by SHARPER FOCUS PUBLISHING division of
SURE FOUNDATION CRT
5671 Polk Drive
Noblesville, IN 46062
www.FromkeBooks.com

Distributed by BOOK DEPOT
11298 Old Paths Lane
Shoals, Indiana 47581-7234

CONTENTS

INTRODUCTION

As I offer this new book for our reading family, my burden is that each of you will sharpen your focus...begin to see and enter into God's calling for your life.

For years after meetings where I have spoken, listeners have come to announce, "Oh, I'm so glad God has a purpose for me."

My response has been, "Yes, He really does, but that was not the focus of my teaching tonight." They are puzzled, until I explain that—in our teaching—we were primarily occupied with Father/God's purpose for Himself. Once we really grasp the wonder of God's purpose for Himself, we will recognize how all other purposes and visions must relate to that...that is DIVINE VISION.

VISION is so important! There are many people who have good eyes, yet they do not have vision.

Helen Keller was once asked, "Is there anything worse than not having your sight?"

She responded earnestly, "Oh yes. It would be much worse to have your sight but not to have vision."

Think of all the opportunities and responsibilities that are lost today because you are too busy looking at what is two feet in front of you.

Many people have dreams...yet do not have vision. Could it be that even our fondest aspirations and goals evaporate like a mist and we are disappointed—because they are merely our own dreams? When God invites us to see from His viewpoint—to see what He is after—then we are truly entering into vision…God's vision! We pray that the lessons of this manual will help you see FATHER'S PURPOSE FOR HIMSELF.

When the Apostle Paul prayed for the *"eyes of your understanding to be enlightened"* he had vision to recognize that God had opened various doors of opportunity:

> *…a great door for effective work is opened to me…*
>   (1 Cor. 16:9 NIV)
> *…a door was opened unto me of the Lord,*
>   (2 Cor. 2:12 KJV)

When we are totally honest, we must confess how much we need God's help in making our quiet times of reading and prayer more effective. We go through the motions, yet inwardly sense there ought to be "something more living…more satisfying."

Could I suggest—it may be there is no sharp focus in your daily pursuits. Answer this: WHY am I living today? How can this day count for eternity? There are scores of good things that can catch our attention and drain away our energy and time.

The pages in this FOCUS MANUAL offer no secret formula for success. We simply remind you that God is "always there!" He is waiting for you to meet Him regularly and He is very active in opening doors of opportunity for those who will diligently seek to "hear His voice…and then obey."

WE WILL MEET YOU EACH DAY AT HIS THRONE… DeVern & Ruth

In earlier years thousands have enjoyed books written by Dr. Walter Wilson. We observed that he moved through each day with unusual sensitivity and expectancy in his soul winning. We have selected this typical incident during one of his visits to New York City. He writes about himself as "the little man in a Big City" who looked for...

AN OPPORTUNITY TO WITNESS

ONE morning before he went out for a business appointment, Dr. Wilson, M.D., prayed in his hotel room, "My Lord, New York is a large city of millions of people, and I am just a weak, unknown servant of Thine with no knowledge of the hungry hearts that may be here. You alone know whom You have been dealing with; here is my body, my feet and my lips. Take me to some troubled heart and speak through me some words of life and light. I believe You will do this." Note his expectancy!

As he walked eastward on 32nd Street, he passed a stationery shop and noticed a small leather-covered notebook in the window. This brought to mind his need of a book in which to keep his prayer list. As he entered the shop he discovered the German owner who showed him the notebook, which was satisfactory in both size and price.

As the shopkeeper began to wrap it up, Dr. Wilson asked, "Do you know what I expect to do with this little book?"

Of course he did not know and was quite astonished to learn that it was to be used as a prayer book. Immediately he began to unwrap the package, explaining, "I am sorry my friend, but this is a blank book. It is not a prayer book."

That was just the opening the doctor needed. He explained that he made his own prayer book, using the left-hand side for petitions and the right-hand side for answers. Then Dr. Wilson added his testimony of knowing the Lord Jesus as his personal Savior. He paused and suggested, "Perhaps you would also like to know Him."

The shopkeeper's response was amazing, "Mister, I have tried to find Gott for many years. I have gone around Manhattan and Brooklyn and the Bronx night after night attending services, but always failed to find Gott. Can you tell me how to get Him?"

After explaining from the Scripture that the Lord Jesus was the Way, the Truth and the Life, the doctor led his new friend to receive Jesus as his Savior. It was the right time for a heart to receive and to rejoice with much thanksgiving! At last the shopkeeper knew the Lord Jesus for himself; his quest of many years had reached its end.

Would you believe only twenty minutes had elapsed from the doctor's prayer in the hotel room to the winning of this soul to Christ?

During the many years that I knew Dr. Wilson and read many similar accounts of soul winning in his books, one thing stands out supremely—He was always expectant that God would prepare him to recognize an OPEN DOOR OF OPPORTUNITY!

I hope you have read some of the books by Watchman Nee of China. Note his exhortation, "New believers should take prayer seriously...each one should prepare a prayer book for listing prayer accounts."

George Müller was another believer serious about prayer. During one year, God answered his prayers three thousand times. How would he know that figure if he had not recorded all of them? "It is a pity that I threw away my old prayer books. To look over those old books would be most interesting. Once I was rather ambitious; I wrote down 140 names in my prayer book. Eighteen months later, all except two were saved. Some names were entered in the morning and they were saved that very afternoon; others were saved after seven or eight months. Once things are recorded in the book, they become business items to be seriously transacted before God. There can be no letup. They must be prayed over and over again, day by day until the transactions are completed.... If our prayers are not answered, something must be drastically wrong. The elderly as well as the young should keep a prayer book."

PONDER THIS PRINCIPLE: When we have finished our life's journey and look back over our lives, each of us will wish we had made more time for prayer. Knowing our weakness and proneness to failure, why not claim this promise right now— *It is God who is at work within you, giving you the will and the power to achieve His purpose.* (Phil. 2:13 Phil)

MEDITATE ON THESE VERSES: *Ask and it will be given to you. Search and you will find. Knock and the door will be opened for you. The one who asks will always receive; the one who is searching will always find, and the door is opened to the man who knocks.* (Matt. 7:7, 8 Phil)

WE PRAY: Father, I am excited about this new door of commitment I am entering. What encourages me most is that You will not only give me the will but the power to continue. Amen!

Daily Focus

_____

_____

_____

_____

_____

_____

_____

_____

_____

Great men know how to seize the moment of opportunity. In fact they usually make opportunities which others do not see. Perhaps there is some secret all of us need to understand! In this lesson we shall consider the power of mutuality. We must see how God in wisdom has designed our cooperation into His plan. We shall see that it is...

NOT YOU...NOR I...BUT WE

THE special evening had finally come. For days a mother had looked forward to the time she and her young son could attend a Paderewski concert. They were about to be seated when the mother spotted an old friend and walked down the aisle to greet her.

Seizing the opportunity to discover the wonders of the concert hall, the little son rose and eventually explored his way through a door marked "NO ADMITTANCE." As the house lights dimmed signaling the concert's beginning, the mother returned to her seat only to discover that her child was missing.

Suddenly, the stage curtains parted revealing the impressive Steinway on which spotlights were focused. And then...she saw him! Sitting at the keyboard was her little son, innocently picking out "Twinkle, Twinkle Little Star."

At that moment, the great piano master made his entrance, quickly moved to the piano, and whispered in the boy's ear, "Don't quit; keep on playing." Then leaning over, Paderewski reached down with his left hand and began filling in the bass notes. Soon his right arm reached around to the other side of the child, and he added a running obbligato.

Together, the old master and the young novice transformed what could have been an awkward situation into a wonderfully creative experience. The audience was so mesmerized that by the end of the concert, they couldn't recall what else the great master played, except for the classic "Twinkle, Twinkle Little Star."

Perhaps that's the way it is with God. What we can accomplish on our own is hardly noteworthy. We try our best, but the results aren't always graceful, flowing music. Thus, we learn the DIVINE SECRET OF MUTUALITY. In that final hour when the GREAT CONCERT OF LIFE will be concluded, we can happily announce it was not me, nor was it Him alone, but it was WE...God and I—together! With His hands enfolding mine and His arms surrounding mine, we can present the MASTERPIECE of Life for all the world to behold.

MUTUALITY! Not I...nor Him...but WE! It has become the focus of all my efforts. The early church fathers were so right when they announced, "The chief end of man is to glorify God (by) enjoying Him forever." It works like this—

when God is honored, then I will also enjoy honor with Him. When He is fully satisfied, then I will also be satisfied. Yes, there is a MUTUAL GLORY yet to unfold!

Have you heard Someone whispering in your ear,

"Don't quit; keep playing.

I don't call the equipped, but I equip the 'called'."

PONDER THIS PRINCIPLE: Life is more accurately measured by the lives you have deeply touched...than by the things you have acquired or the goals you have achieved.

MEDITATE ON THIS VERSE: *Before long, the world will not see Me anymore, but you will see Me. Because I live, you also will live. On that day you will realize I am in my Father, and you are in Me, and I am in you.* (John 14:19, 20 NIV)

WE PRAY: Father, I want to recognize You as the One who invites us to participate in Your Ultimate Intention. I want to be submissive—willing and always joyfully anticipating the unveiling of YOUR FINAL MASTERPIECE. I can hardly wait for that day when all creation will bow and acknowledge YOU ARE WORTHY. Then with one gesture You will point to Your Lovely Son...and sons, to announce,

"THE WHOLE WORLD IS FILLED WITH HIS GLORY."

Daily Focus

We face this question: Is it proper to help someone reach significance, even though in the natural order they have some very real limitations? We shall see in this story how the principle of mutuality brings great blessing to all who participate. In that final day when all God's purposes have been fulfilled, Our Father will make the glorious announcement, "In My family...

ALL MY CHILDREN WIN

A FATHER was speaking at a fundraising dinner for a school that serves learning-disabled children. After extolling the school and its dedicated staff, he tenderly spoke of his own son, Shay, who was physically and mentally handicapped. He offered the question shared above and then told the following story:

Shay and his father had walked past a baseball game where some boys Shay knew were playing. Shay asked, "Do you think they'll let me play?" Shay's father knew that most of the boys would not want someone like Shay on their team, but he also understood that if his son were allowed to play it would give him a much-needed sense of belonging and some confidence to be accepted by others in spite of his handicaps.

Shay's father approached one of the boys on the field and asked if Shay could play, not expecting much. The boy looked around for guidance and said, "We're losing by six runs and the game is in the eighth inning. I guess he can be on our team and we'll try to put him in to bat in the ninth inning."

Shay struggled over to the team's bench and pulled on a team shirt with a broad smile. His father had a small tear in his eye and warmth in his heart; the boys saw the father's joy at their acceptance of his son. In the bottom of the eighth inning, Shay's team scored a few runs but was still behind by three. In the top of the ninth inning, Shay put on a glove and played in the right field. Even though no hits came his way, he was obviously ecstatic just to be in the game and on the field, grinning from ear to ear as his father waved to him from the stands. In the bottom of the ninth inning Shay's team scored again. Now, with two outs and the bases loaded, the potential winning run was on base and—Shay was scheduled to be next at bat.

It was a critical moment! Would they let Shay bat and give away their chance to win the game? Surprisingly, Shay was given the bat. Everyone knew that a hit was all but impossible because Shay didn't even know how to hold the bat properly, much less connect with the ball. However, as Shay stepped up to the plate, the pitcher, recognizing the other team had put winning aside for this moment in Shay's life, moved in a few steps to lob the ball softly so Shay could at least make contact. The first pitch came and Shay swung clumsily and missed. The pitcher again took a few steps forward to toss the ball gently towards Shay. As the pitch came in, Shay swung at the ball and hit a slow ground ball right back to the pitcher.

The game would now be over, as the pitcher picked up the soft grounder which could easily be thrown to the first baseman. Shay would have been out, ending the game; instead, the pitcher lobbed the ball high over the head of the first baseman, out of reach of all teammates. Everyone from the stands and both teams began yelling, "Shay, run to first! Run to first!" Never in his life had Shay run that far, but he scampered down the baseline, wide-eyed and startled, making it to first base. Then everyone yelled, "Run to second, run to second!"

By the time Shay rounded towards second base, the right fielder had the ball—the smallest guy on their team who had a chance to be his team's hero for the first time. He could have thrown the ball to the second baseman for the tag, but he understood the pitcher's intentions and he, too, threw the ball high and far over the second baseman's head. Shay ran toward the base deliriously as the runners ahead of him circled the bases toward home. All were screaming, "Shay, Shay, Shay, all the way, Shay."

When Shay reached second base, the opposing shortstop ran to help him and turned him in the direction of third base then shouted, "Run to third Shay, run to third!" As Shay rounded third, the boys from both teams and those watching were on their feet screaming for Shay to keep running. Shay ran to home, stepped on the plate and was cheered as the hero who hit the "grand slam" and won the game for his team.

"That day," said his father softly with tears now rolling down his face, "the boys from both teams helped bring a piece of true love and mutuality into this world."

Shay didn't make it to another summer. He died that winter, having never forgotten being the hero, making his father so happy, then receiving his mother's tearful embrace for her little champion!

PONDER THIS PRINCIPLE: It is in God's planning that we all enjoy an identity of who we are in our relationship to Our Father and His family. Also we can enjoy some significance in what we have become as we finish life's race. Finally, (as it was with Shay) we can experience true mutuality through how we relate to others in helping them fulfill their final destinies. Let us not forget the importance of identity, significance and mutuality.

It was in our Father's planning that He would limit His own sovereignty in order to allow man freedom to choose. The interplay between this tension of God's will and man's will allows God to bring each of His children to joyfully embrace the will of God as his own will. What a victory! In that final day Father can announce to all the universe it was not what I did, or what you did, but what WE DID. THAT IS

THE GLORY OF ULTIMATE MUTUALITY. Everyone in God's family wins!

MEDITATE ON THESE VERSES: *When I think of the greatness of this great plan I fall on my knees before the Father (from whom all fatherhood, earthly and heavenly, derives its name), and I pray that out of the glorious riches of His resources He will enable you to know glorious richness...that Christ may actually live in your hearts by your faith...and to know for yourselves that love so far beyond our comprehension. May you be filled through all your being with God Himself...to Him be glory in the Church and in Christ Jesus for ever and ever. Amen.* (Eph. 3:14-19 Phil)

WE PRAY: Father, may all that the Apostle Paul prayed for the saints—our identity, our significance, and our mutuality—be fully realized for Your glory. Amen

Daily Focus

_____

_____

_____

_____

_____

_____

_____

_____

When we start with God's creative plan before the beginning, it is important to consider the following questions: Was it necessary for Adam to sin—so God could add a redemptive plan? If Adam had not sinned, what was God's plan for bringing him to maturity of character? Or was he already mature when he came from the creative hand of God? So we ask, what was our...

FATHER'S ORIGINAL PURPOSE

WHILE we must never minimize the redemptive plan of God, we must be careful not to allow it to overshadow God's original Paternal Plan which He determined before the beginning. It is important to realize God did have a plan and purpose for Adam before his insurrection in the garden. It was not necessary for Adam to sin! That would make God responsible for sin...God forbid!

The scriptures are clear—God has now so wonderfully incorporated His redemptive plan, that many folk have not distinguished the original creative plan from the redemptive plan which has now been added. Perhaps without realizing it, many have been living in the smaller box (redemption) when they should be living in the larger perspective of God's ultimate intention.

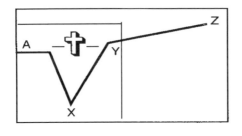 As we have pictured in the diagram, Adam could have yielded himself to God and chosen to move on the line of God's eternal purpose (A to Z). But, as he stood at the door of opportunity (A) Adam made a bad choice. Adam "turned to his own way" (A to X) rather than choosing God's way (A to Z). Now Adam needs God's redemption through the Cross (X to Y, thus the "Redemptive Box"). (For further insights on this, see the author's earlier book, THE ULTIMATE INTENTION.)

What might have been the result if Adam had not sinned, but had made the right choice, we will now consider. Several writers have offered their conclusions:

> It is a governing principle of God's working—first
> the natural and then the spiritual. So it was in God's
> design that Adam was created as a natural man.
> The first Adam was God's best work by creation.
> However, it was God's original plan that through
> obedience Adam should transform the natural into
> spiritual. That is all we can say. Now, because of
> Adam's disobedience many things have changed.
> So, fallen man must trust Christ to be redeemed,
> i.e. forgiven. Actually that moves one back to

where Adam started; he needs more than forgiveness, he also needs Divine Life. So, in receiving Christ as his Life, he now becomes a child of God by divine begetting. Many would stop here, but God's design is that through continued obedience redeemed Adam should enter into mature sonship...which comes by the painful process of character development. (OC, ed. DF)
In the beginning God had a wonderful purpose for man to fulfill. As Adam came from the creative hand of God he was perfect—yet not completed in his moral character. To become a mature person requires that one make choices—i.e. pass through testing that will develop character. God had planned that man might not only "be" but also "become" a vital participant, who could "share" in God's coming Kingdom which will one day be established. (CAJ)

You are made to grow. The creative God made you for creative growth. Growth is the law of your being. Violate that law, and you violate yourself. You are unfulfilled; hence you become frustrated and unhappy. On the other hand, when you are fulfilling the law of your being as a growing personality...this spreads central satisfaction through all the marginal happenings of life. Whether these happenings are unhappy or not, you are centrally happy. While you do not seek happiness, it is the by-product of a mature, growing personality. (ESJ)

PONDER THIS: Only in recent years has there been an awakening to see the importance of moving from the Redemptive Box to live in the larger Purpose Box. As long as I live in the Redemptive Box I am primarily alive to getting all "my inheritance in Christ." That is important! But when I move into the Purpose Box I become alive to God's ultimate intention. Then, I become more alive to "God's inheritance in the saints." Yes, both are very important.

GOD'S WORD: When the apostle Paul wrote to the saints at Ephesus, he reminded them of *"OUR inheritance"* in Christ (1:14); then he realized they needed enlargement. So he prayed that their eyes would be enlightened to see *"...the glory of HIS inheritance in the saints"* (1:18 KJV). It is possible that the Ephesian saints were like many of us, who have recognized "OUR inheritance" but have mostly missed "HIS inheritance." That is why Paul prayed so earnestly for them.

Now consider this: the basis for receiving OUR inheritance in Christ is because of His death on the Cross. And the basis of God receiving HIS inheritance in the saints is simply that we "die to our own selfish plans and ambitions."

WE PRAY: Father, with the apostle Paul we bow with a heart of thanksgiving. You have shown us how a self-centered pre-occupation with what we get can keep us from being wholly God-centered—i.e. always alive to what You receive from our lives. OH...make that radical adjustment in us now.

Daily Focus

_____

_____

_____

_____

_____

_____

_____

_____

_____

_____

_____

_____

_____

_____

_____

_____

_____

_____

John Powell, a professor at Loyola University in Chicago writes about a student named Tommy in his "Theology of Faith" class. He wisely answered Tommy when he posed a cynical question. This story reveals that it was God at work, waiting for the right moment to awaken Tommy to his deepest need. Professor Powell's unusual response to Tommy's question was...

GOD WILL FIND YOU!

SOME twelve years ago, I stood watching my university students file into the classroom for our first session in the Theology of Faith class. That was the day I first saw Tommy. My eyes and mind both blinked. He was combing his long flaxen hair, which hung six inches below his shoulders. It was the first time I had ever seen a boy with hair that long; I guess it was just coming into fashion then. I know in my mind that it's not what's on your head but what's in it that counts, but on that day I was unprepared and my emotions flipped. I immediately filed Tommy under "S" for strange, very strange.

Tommy turned out to be the "atheist in residence" in my Theology of Faith course. He constantly objected to, smirked at or whined about the possibility of an unconditionally loving Father/God. We lived with each other in relative peace for one semester, although I admit he was for me, at times, a serious pain in the back pew.

As he turned in his final exam at the end of the course, he asked in a slightly cynical tone, "Do you think I'll ever find God?"

I decided instantly on a little shock therapy. "No!" I said very emphatically.

"Oh," he responded, "I thought that was the product you were pushing."

I let him get five steps from the classroom door then called out, "Tommy! I don't think you'll ever find Him, but I am absolutely certain that He will find you!"

He shrugged a little and left my class and my life. I felt slightly disappointed at the thought that he had missed my clever line, "He will find you!" At least I thought it was clever.

Later, I heard that Tommy had graduated, and I was duly grateful. Then a sad report came. I heard Tommy had terminal cancer. Before I could search him out, he came to see me. When he walked into my office his body was badly wasted. Chemotherapy had resulted in his long hair falling out, but his eyes were bright and his voice was firm for the first time, I believe.

"Tommy, I've thought about you so often. I hear you are sick," I blurted.

"Oh, yes, very sick; I have cancer in both lungs. It's a matter of weeks."

"Can you talk about it, Tom?" I asked.

"Sure, what would you like to know?" he replied.

"What's it like to be only twenty-four and dying?"

"Well, it could be worse."

"Like what?"

"Well, like being fifty and having no values or ideals; like being fifty and thinking that booze, seducing women, and making money are the real 'biggies' in life."

(I began to look through my mental file cabinet under "S" where I had filed Tommy as strange. It seems as though everybody I try to reject by classification, God sends back into my life to educate me.)

"But what I really came to see you about," Tom said, "is something you said to me on the last day of class." (He remembered!) He continued, "I asked you if you thought I would ever find God, and you said, 'No!' which surprised me. Then you said, 'But He will find you.' I thought about that a lot, even though my search for God was hardly intense at that time."

(My clever line...He thought about that a lot!)

"When the doctors removed a lump from my groin and told me that it was malignant, that's when I got serious about locating God. And when the malignancy spread into my vital organs I really began banging bloody fists against the bronze doors of heaven, but God did not come out. In fact, nothing happened. Did you ever try something for a long time with great effort and with no success? You get psychologically glutted—fed up with trying. And then you quit.

"Well, one day I woke up....and instead of throwing a few more futile appeals over that high brick wall to a God who may or may not be there, I just quit. I decided that I didn't really care about God, about an afterlife, or anything like that. I decided to spend what time I had left doing something more profitable.

"Then I thought about you and your class, and I remembered something else you had said, 'The essential sadness is to go through life without loving. But it would be almost equally sad to go through life and leave this world without ever telling those you loved that you had loved them.'

"So, I determined to tell them. I began with the hardest one, my Dad. He was reading the newspaper when I approached him.

"Dad."

"Yes, what?" he asked without lowering the newspaper.

"Dad, I would like to talk with you."

"Well...talk."

"I mean it's really important."

The newspaper came down three slow inches. "What is it?"

"Dad, I love you. I just wanted you to know that."

(Tom smiled at me and said it with obvious satisfaction, as though he felt a warm and secret joy flowing inside of him.)

"The newspaper fluttered to the floor. Then my father did two things I couldn't remember him ever doing before. He cried and he hugged me. We talked all night, even though he had to go to work the next morning. It felt so good to be close to my father, to see his tears, to feel his hug, to hear him say that he loved me.

"It was easier to tell my mother and little brother. They cried with me, too, and we hugged each other, and started saying really nice things to each other. We shared many things we had been keeping secret for years.

"I was only sorry about one thing—that I had waited so long. Here I was, just beginning to open up to all these people I had actually been close to.

"Then, one day, I turned around...and God was there! He didn't come to me when I pleaded with Him. I guess I was like an animal trainer holding out a hoop, 'C'mon, jump through. C'mon, I'll give you three days, three weeks.' Apparently God does things in His own way and His own time. But the important thing is that He was there. HE FOUND ME! You were right. He found me even after I stopped looking for Him."

"Tommy," I practically gasped, "I think you are saying something very important and much more universal than you realize. To me, at least, you are saying that the surest way to find God is not to make Him a private possession, a problem solver, or an instant consolation in time of need, but rather to open up to love. You know, the Apostle John said, 'God is love, and anyone who lives in love is living with God and God is living in him.'

"Tom, could I ask you a favor? You know, when I had you in class you were a real pain. But (laughingly) you can make it all up to me now. Would you come into my present Theology of Faith course and tell them what you have just told me? If I told them the same thing it wouldn't be half as effective as if you were to tell them."

"Ooh...I was ready for you, but I don't know if I'm ready for your class."

"Tom, think about it. If and when you are ready, give me a call."

In a few days Tom called saying he was ready for the class...that he wanted to do that for God and for me. So we scheduled a date, but he never made it. He had another appointment far more important than the one with my class and me.

Of course, Tom's life was not really ended by his death, only changed. Before he died, we talked one last time.

"I'm not going to make it to your class," he said.

"I know, Tom."

"Will you tell them for me? Will you tell the whole world for me?"

"I will, Tom. I'll tell them. I'll do my best."

So, to all of you who have been kind enough to read this simple statement about love, thank you. And to you, Tommy,—I told them, yes, Tommy,—as best I could. (Professor John Powell)

This touching story and its satisfying resolution are very significant. We accept his testimony that Tommy did indeed trust the finished work of Christ for his own salvation even though Tommy did not express his faith in our terminology. As evangelicals we must be careful to recognize that God honors the government of the heart when it yields to Him, even though one's spiritual understanding might be incomplete or different.

I have selected this story because it speaks to our hearts, but it also uncovers a misunderstanding of love and a dangerous trend in our day. William Kelly warns, "(Today) one of the main things we have to guard against is Satan's endeavoring to persuade people that, because God is love, therefore love is God.

"It is not so! If I say that God is love, I bring out what He is in the active energy of His holy nature. But this is not all that God is. He is light as much as He is love, and I must own His love without the denial of His light. What prevails among many now is the deifying of love (*as a principle*) but it strips God of His light." (*and His Personhood—author*)

I wish we had more professors who would send a prophetic word to awaken other "Tommy's" and penetrate through the hardened defenses. GOD WILL FIND YOU! It is amazing how Tommy could not forget those words—words directed by the Holy Spirit.

If there is failure and paralysis in our service for the Lord, I am convinced it is because we do not see both spiritual fruit (patience) and spiritual gifting (prophetic word)—as demonstrated by Professor Powell. May God help us to lay aside any hidden prejudices.

PONDER THIS PRINCIPLE: When spiritual Life comes to us, it brings Light, and Light always brings Love. This is the divine sequence as we see in the Apostle John's writing. Actually these three are inseparable. Once I receive CHRIST as my Life, I should have a whole new perspective (Light), which helps me to appreciate (Love) others just as He does. It is dangerous to assume that one can truly love—without first having His Life.

MEDITATE ON THESE VERSES: John writes, *In Him was Life and the Life was the Light of men.* (John 1:4 NKJV)... *He that says he is in the light, and hates his brother, is in darkness...he that loves his brother abides in light...* (1 John 2:9, 10 NKJV) When God has His way in us we enjoy His Life-Light-Love in an ever-increasing way.

WE PRAY: Father/God I am willing for personal inventory. Please uncover any hidden prejudices in me that would limit my being more fruitful. I will make room for both the fruit and the gifts of the Spirit as You enable me with Your grace.

Daily Focus

Hopelessness needs to be understood if we are to help anyone. When Victor Frankl was released from imprisonment following the Nazi Holocaust he wrote the book, *Man's Search for Meaning*. He set about to explain one vital thing he had discovered from his suffering: "There is nothing in the world that would so effectively help one survive even the worst conditions as the knowledge that there is a (divine meaning) or...

FOCUS TO ONE'S LIFE

SOME years ago a wise counselor, whom I greatly admire for his work with youth in their conflicts, was invited to a girls' detention center. He asked the prison official for permission to speak briefly with several of the inmates and it was granted.

As each girl approached, he asked her: "If I could help you find some real purpose and meaning for your life, and then you could give yourself to helping other girls around you, would you be interested?" As he recognized their pattern of hopeless reasoning, he quickly followed with another question, "I know you are aware of your weakness, but if you could receive the POWER necessary to make this possible, would you accept the offer?

Without any hesitation each girl responded, "Yes, I would!"

The officials who observed each girl enter the room and exit saw an amazing change in their countenance. They insisted on knowing what the counselor had shared with each girl that brought such manifest change of attitude.

He explained how he had touched the most significant issue in every girl's life—the need for meaning and purpose and her ability to perform. Each girl had quickly given her response because it brought a new FOCUS...turning from one's self-relating to helping others. That gives new HOPE.

So our daily focus should be:
....in making Him known...we know Him better,
....in representing Him...we learn His ways,
....in delighting ourselves in Him...we are contagious!

When we look into our Bibles we recognize how many were sustained when they experienced repeated suffering. We are convinced this divine sense of purpose sustained Joseph in his years of imprisonment in Egypt. It surely sustained Daniel when he faced the jealousy of co-leaders resulting in his being cast into the lions' den.

The Apostle Paul speaks of the life-purpose that sustained him. He told the leaders of the Ephesian church, *"Now I go bound in the spirit to Jerusalem, not knowing the things that will happen to me there, except that the Holy Spirit testifies in every city saying that chains and tribulation await me. But none of these things move me, nor do I count my life dear to myself, so that I may finish my race with joy and the ministry which I have received from the Lord Jesus..."* (Acts 20:22-24 NKJV)

In Romans 1:1 Paul explains this three-fold calling of God for him:

...the general calling...as a bond-servant

...the special calling...to be sent as an apostle, and

...the specific calling...to write letters to the churches.

Consider this three-fold unfolding in the life of Joseph:

...general calling....servant in Potiphar's house

....special calling...interpreter of dreams

....specific calling...governor of Egypt (savior).

Consider this three-fold unfolding in the life of Daniel:

....general calling...servant with a single heart

...special calling...intercessor (ruler of kingdom)

...specific calling...interpreter of God's purposes.

Perhaps this is what God expects from each of us as we press toward a similar fulfillment in our lives.

We have been showing how only a life-purpose will sustain you when you are confronted with crisis situations that seem impossible. It takes more than a clever slogan such as, "Tough times never last, but tough people do," or, "There's a YES in every MESS!" But they get our attention!

Why do some folk conquer while others cave in? As long as the girls in the detention center had no hope, they tended to be bitter and incorrigible. Yet even a ray of hope for a life-purpose seemed to change them immediately. Your life-purpose is given to you by God, but it unfolds as you diligently walk with Him.

Many of you who read this are not sure just how your sense of purpose came, but you know you have a set of divinely inspired convictions chiseled into the bedrock of your soul by His grace. You are already aware of their sustaining power.

PONDER THIS PRINCIPLE: There is no such thing as a totally negative event or experience that cannot end as a positive. There is a YES buried somewhere in your mess. Someone now reading this feels he can get no lower, that he (or she) has blown it and that God could never lift you up and make you profitable again. Let me ask—is God's redeeming power selective? Does He choose to help some because they are more worthy, and cast others aside for the trash heap? Reject your feelings...and the Enemy's lies!

GOD'S WORD: Many years ago I was liberated from negativism when I saw this, *Whatever God has promised gets stamped the Yes of Jesus. In Him, this is what we preach and pray, the great Amen. God's Yes and our Yes together, gloriously evident. God affirms us, making us a sure thing in Christ, putting his Yes within us. By His Spirit*

He has stamped us with His eternal pledge—a sure
beginning of what He is destined to complete. (2 Cor. 1:20
Msg)

WE PRAY: Lord, we are convinced. You will fulfill Your glory
through us...as we keep our eyes fixed upon You and our
hearts delighting in You. Amen!

Daily Focus

_____
_____
_____
_____
_____
_____
_____
_____
_____
_____
_____
_____
_____
_____
_____
_____
_____
_____

God has given to each of us certain talents which we can selfishly squander or conversely yield to God for His use. This total yielding of ourselves for God's purposes is called personal consecration. We should not be surprised that God will arrange an...

OPPORTUNITY TO DEMONSTRATE

SOME years ago a professor of philosophy at USC was widely known as a committed atheist. His primary goal in one of the required classes was to spend the entire semester attempting to prove that God did not exist. Because of his (seemingly) impeccable logic and grandiose manner his students avoided argumentation.

For twenty years he had taught this class. Extremely few students had ever had the courage to challenge him. Although some had openly questioned him in class no one had ever boldly challenged his position because of his reputation.

It had been his custom the last day of every semester to tell the class of 300 students, "If there is anyone here who still believes in God, stand up!" It is almost unbelievable, but in twenty years no student had ever stood up, for they had already heard what he was going to do next. He would insist, "Anyone who believes in God is a fool. If God really existed He could stop this piece of chalk from hitting the floor and breaking. It is such a simple task for Him to prove that He exists. But He never does." Every year the professor would then drop the chalk onto the floor of the classroom and it would shatter into a hundred pieces. That seemed to be the proof he needed!

It is sad how many students from their silence apparently agreed that God didn't exist. Yes, it is likely that some timid Christians had silently slipped through the course. But for twenty years students had been too afraid to stand up and accept the ridicule and the scorn.

Then it happened! One Christian freshman found it necessary to enroll in this course because it was a required for his major. He had already heard the stories about this professor. During the three months of that semester he diligently prayed every morning that God would grant him the courage to stand up no matter what the class thought. He was determined to honor God...determined that nothing he heard would ever shatter his faith.

Finally the last day of the course arrived. The professor in his traditional manner announced, "If there is anyone here who still believes in God, stand up!" Without any hesitation this freshman seated at the back of the classroom stood up. The professor and 300 students looked on in awe and total amazement.

The professor shouted at him, "You FOOL! If God really exists He will keep this piece of chalk from breaking when it hits the floor." Then as he lifted the chalk and proceeded to drop it...it slipped out of his fingers...off his shirt cuff...onto the pleat of his pants, down his leg...and off his shoe. As it reached the floor...it simply rolled away unbroken.

The professor's jaw dropped! There was total silence! He stared down at the chalk. He looked up at the young man... and without saying one word ran out of the lecture hall.

That young freshman who had dared to stand quietly walked to the front of the class and shared his faith in the Lord Jesus for the next half hour. There was a sense of awe, amazing respect and honor as 300 students listened while he explained God's redemptive work for him and for them through the death of Jesus Christ on the cross.

Here was a moment of divine encounter. Each student realized that God had spoken. God does know how to silence His enemies. Perhaps the greater lesson to all of us is that God is ever looking for those who will dare to stand with Him...those who will allow God to speak through them. It was a consecration boldly demonstrated. Who can doubt God had opened this door—an opportunity for a young freshman to become His voice in that classroom?

I wrote in the back of my Bible almost fifty years ago, "There is a boldness of the flesh that disgusts but there is a boldness of the Spirit that disarms." I feel sure God looked down that day and said, "It is time to accept the bold challenge of this professor." How simple it was for Him to cause his clumsy fingers to lose the chalk before he could drop it. We are claiming this intervention was a door of opportunity for the young man to become an authentic voice for God.

Recall that this freshman had prayed every morning during that semester for wisdom and God's supply of grace. This was not some bold whim of the flesh; his boldness was by God's enablement.

PONDER THIS PRINCIPLE: Our Lord was gripped by a master ambition that integrated the whole of His life. It can be summarized in a single sentence, *I have come to do Your will, O God* (Heb. 10:7 NIV). When He offered His wonderful high-priestly prayer at life's end, He was able to report the complete achievement of this ambition, *I have brought You glory on earth by completing the work You gave Me to do.* (John 17:4 NIV)

MEDITATE ON THESE VERSES: *When a man's ways are pleasing to the Lord, He makes even his enemies live at peace with him.... In his heart a man plans his course, but the Lord determines his steps* (Proverbs 16:7, 9 NIV)

WE PRAY: Father, we know that when any man speaks it must be Your voice that is heard. We know it is wrong to hastily reject the opinion of fellow-workers, but it is also wrong to accept their opinions as a substitute for the direct witness of Your Spirit to our spirit. While we must never be independent of the other members of the Body, help us never forget that it is from our Head that all our direction comes.

Daily Focus

_____
_____
_____
_____
_____
_____
_____
_____
_____
_____
_____
_____
_____
_____
_____
_____
_____
_____
_____
_____

When we want to impress kids (or anyone) we invite some well-known celebrity to speak who gives a bold testimony of how many things changed when he gave his life to Christ. Everyone admires such a hero, and rightly so. Yet, when God looks for someone He can use...

HE WORKS DIFFERENTLY

TONY CAMPOLO explains this difference:

I was asked to be a counselor in a junior high camp. Everybody ought to be a counselor in a junior high camp—just once!

A junior high kid's concept of a good time is picking on people. And in this particular case, at this particular camp, there was a little boy who was suffering from cerebral palsy; his name was Billy. And they picked on him. Oh, they picked on him. As he walked across the camp with his uncoordinated body they would line up and imitate his grotesque movements. I watched him one day as he was asking for direction. "Which...way is...the...craft...shop?" he stammered, his mouth contorting.

And the boys mimicked in that same awful stammer. "It's...over...there...Billy." And then they laughed at him. I was irate.

But my furor reached its highest pitch when on Thursday morning it was Billy's cabin's turn to give devotions. I wondered what would happen, because they appointed Billy to be the speaker. I knew that they just wanted to get him up there to make fun of him. As he dragged his way to the front, you could hear the giggles rolling over the crowd. It took little Billy almost five minutes to say seven words, "Jesus...loves...me...and...I love...Jesus."

When he finished, there was dead silence. I looked over my shoulder and saw junior high boys bawling all over the place. A revival broke out in that camp after Billy's short testimony. As I travel all over the world, to this day, I find missionaries and preachers who say, "Remember me? I was converted at that junior high camp."

We counselors had tried everything to get those kids interested in Jesus. We even imported baseball players whose batting averages had gone up since they had started praying. But God chose not to use the superstars. He chose a kid with cerebral palsy to break the spirits of the haughty. He's that kind of God...and His ways are often so different.

Consider others God has used. God called a timid man with a stutter—a speech impediment—by the name of Moses, who became one of the greatest leaders in the Old Testament. God called David, a little shepherd boy, right out of the pasture and made him one of the greatest kings who ruled over Israel.

Consider Jonathan Edwards one of the greatest revival preachers America has known. He was asthmatic. When he stood to preach he would hack and wheeze during most of his message. He was a very thin, frail man with horrible eyesight—surely not very charismatic. Despite all these disabilities, Jonathan Edwards' sermons caused people to come down the aisle writhing in anguish wanting to get right with God. If you wonder why there was an amazing anointing on this man, history records that when Jonathan was eighteen years old he wrote, "If there could be one man in the world at one time who was pleasing to God, I would want to be that man."

Consider why the Apostle Paul wrote, ...*not many wise...not many noble...But God hath chosen the foolish things of this world to confound the wise; and God hath chosen the weak things of this world to...bring to nought things that are...He that glorieth let him glory in the Lord.* (1 Cor. 1:26-31 KJV)

What is the difference? The anointing! It is like a hammer that breaks any hardness; it is like a light that exposes the darkness. What human might and power cannot do, the Holy Spirit's anointing can accomplish.

One day at a conference, Dr. C. I. Scofield's voice filled with righteous indignation as he explained, "People say that the bird with the broken pinion never soars as high again, as if we did not all have a broken wing! For most of us both wings are broken and both legs, and our necks! So let us give up this notion that it is the 'broken pinion' that is going to keep us from soaring as high as some victorious Christians can soar. One thing is certain—a bird <u>without</u> a broken pinion is never going to be used greatly for God." This sounds so strange to modern ears when we insist God makes no offer of fruitfulness to strong people, only to people who have failed utterly—and come to total weakness.

PONDER THIS PRINCIPLE: God's work in the past has been done by ordinary run-of-the-mill people who become a polished shaft in His hand. He is still looking for the same today!

MEDITATE ON THIS VERSE: *God has chosen what the world counts folly, and to shame what is strong God has chosen what the world counts weakness. He has chosen things low and contemptible, mere nothings, to overthrow the existing order. And so there is no place for human pride in the presence of God.* (1 Cor. 1: 28 NEB)

WE PRAY: Father, when I am totally honest, I realize I do want to become a polished shaft in Your hand, but I also realize I am not willing for such a dealing. Lord, I ask You to develop in me a willingness to be willing...

Daily Focus

In the course of our daily activity we often face opportunities to "be like Jesus." It is interesting that Jesus never seemed rushed or out-of-breath. He was never feverishly hurrying to His next appointment, though He was committed to fulfilling life's most important work—His Father's! How much we need to understand...

ALWAYS BEING AVAILABLE

A FEW years ago a group of salesmen went to a regional sales convention in Chicago. They had assured their wives they would be home in plenty of time for Friday night's dinner.

In their rush with tickets and briefcases, one of these salesmen inadvertently kicked over a table that held a display of apples. Apples flew everywhere. Without stopping or looking back, they all managed to reach the gate in time for their nearly missed boarding—all but one. He paused, took a deep breath, got in touch with his feelings, and experienced a twinge of compassion for the girl whose apple stand had been overturned.

He told his buddies to go on without him. As he waved goodbye he told one of them to call his wife when he arrived home and explain that he was taking a later flight. Then he returned to the place where the apples were spilled all over the terminal floor.

He was glad he did.

The 16-year-old girl was totally blind. She was softly crying, tears running down her cheeks in frustration, and at the same time helplessly groping for her spilled produce as the crowd swirled about her. No one stopped or seemed to care for her plight.

The salesman knelt down on the floor with her, gathered up the apples, put them into the baskets and helped set the display up once more. As he did this, he noticed that many of the apples had become battered and bruised; these he set aside in another basket.

When he had finished, he pulled out his wallet and said to the girl, "Here, please take this $20 for the damage we did. Are you okay?" She nodded through her tears. He continued, "I hope we didn't spoil your day too badly."

As the salesman started to walk away, the bewildered blind girl called out to him, "Mister..." He paused and turned to look back into those blind eyes. She asked, "Are you Jesus?"

Today I know how much we emphasize keeping our promises, and in business fulfilling our goals. But, whose goals? Oh that we can once-for-all settle the fact that we are first of all called to be...

Available for eternal issues,
Adjustable to His ways,
Accountable to Him.

I know what you are thinking! Is it conceivable that we should take time to clean up a mess made by another? Is it possible to pick up every basket of spilled apples? No, of course not. That is why we must develop an ear to hear His voice. He alone can help us discern our steps and our stops. Today there are so many things crying out for our attention. Yes, there is an answer!

PONDER THIS PRINCIPLE: There are many voices around us calling out for help. The more sensitive we become in developing a servant spirit, the more we will need to recognize the distinctive quality of His voice.

Many years ago I sat in a prayer circle in Bradenton, Florida. A farmer, who had just retired from his farm, told how his flock of sheep had been loaded into a truck. He loved them so much; it was heart-rending to part with them. As one final gesture of love he decided to follow them to the railroad yards where they would be herded into boxcars. He wondered how they would be treated and how much they would miss him.

When he found the railroad siding where his sheep were loaded, he and his wife walked down the tracks shouting his love to them and singing a song he had often sung. I watched this man's face as he explained, "Would you believe in that vast area of loaded freight we finally heard the bleating from one car? The closer we got the more the bleating increased."

He explained that he and his wife stood there singing...and weeping. Then he announced, "I understand now why our Lord Jesus insisted, 'My sheep know My voice.'"

MEDITATE ON THIS VERSE: *So we thy people and the sheep of thy pasture will give thee thanks forever: we will shew forth thy praise to all generations.* (Psa. 79:13 KJV)

WE PRAY: When we think of how our Lord Jesus was the Perfect Lamb, we announce that our desire is to BE LIKE HIM. Perhaps in that way the blind of this world will see through our loving actions that we are like Him. And they will ask, "Are you Jesus?"

Daily Focus

_____

_____

_____

_____

_____

_____

_____

_____

_____

_____

_____

_____

_____

_____

_____

We know by experience that when God opens a door of opportunity for us today, we must be adjustable if we would extend our compassion to some person in deep need. Usually it will cost us...

A LITTLE TIME AND PRIDE

THIS true story will speak to your heart. It comes from a mother of three who recently completed her college degree. She explains that her last class was Sociology:

Our teacher was most inspiring, embodying the qualities with which I wish every human had been graced. Her last project of the term was called "SMILE." She asked the members of the class to go out and smile at three people and document their reactions. Since I am a very friendly person with a ready smile, I thought this would be a piece of cake. Soon afterwards on a crisp March morning, my husband took our youngest son and me to McDonald's for breakfast.

Standing in line waiting to be served, all of a sudden I sensed everyone around me backing away, even my husband. I did not move an inch, but a feeling of panic welled up inside as I turned to see why they had moved.

Then...I smelled a horrible 'dirty body' smell, and there standing behind me were two poor homeless men. As I looked down at the short gentleman closest to me, he was 'smiling.' His beautiful sky blue eyes were full of light as he searched for acceptance. Then he spoke a soft, "Good day," as he counted the few coins he had been clutching. The second man behind him was obviously mentally challenged and it was evident he depended on his friend. I held my tears as I stood there with them. The young lady at the counter asked him what he wanted.

"Coffee is all, Miss!" was his reply, because apparently that was all he could afford. The restaurant provided a much-needed haven to sit and warm up, but a purchase was required to do so.

As they walked to a table, I felt a strong compulsion; it was so great I almost reached out and embraced the little man with blue eyes. Suddenly I noticed all eyes in the restaurant were set on me—judging my every action.

I smiled and asked the young lady to give me two more breakfast meals on a separate tray. Walking around the corner to the men's table, I put the tray down and covered the blue-eyed gentleman's cold hand with mine. Tears sprang to his eyes as he murmured his thanks. I began to pat his hand and said, "I did this because God is here working through me to give you hope."

I started to cry as I walked away to join my husband and son. When I sat down my husband smiled at me and said, "That is why God gave you to me, Honey, to give me hope." We held hands for a moment and knew that only because of the Grace we had been given were we able to give.

I returned with this story in hand for my last evening class. The instructor read it and then asked, "Can I share this?" I slowly nodded as she got the attention of the class. She began to read and that is when I knew that we as human beings need to love with God's love and be available to heal people and be healed. In my own way I realized I had touched the people at McDonald's, my son, my husband, instructor, and every soul that shared the classroom on the last night I spent as a college student.

In my graduation I was awakened to one of the greatest lessons I would ever learn—to give UNCONDITIONAL ACCEPTANCE. As a recipient of God's boundless love and grace, I'm also called to be His representative of those very qualities no matter whom I encounter.

PONDER THIS PRINCIPLE: We know that our own love will not stoop to help someone unlovely. Our love soon runs out. We must be convinced that God's love (agape) will flow through us. But it must be our determined focus to love people and use things, not use people and love things.

MEDITATE ON THIS VERSE: *Be kindly affectionate to one another with brotherly love...given to hospitality.* (Rom.12:10, 13 NKJV) This means whether or not I feel like it, and whether or not they seem worthy.

WE PRAY: Father, would You please help me to become more sensitive to the needs of others? I really need discernment to know when You are nudging me, and when it is just my own imagination. I believe I am learning to recognize YOUR VOICE.

Daily Focus

_____

_____

_____

_____

_____

_____

_____

_____

_____

_____

_____

_____

_____

_____

_____

_____

_____

_____

_____

_____

_____

_____

In recent years the world has acknowledged the passing of Mother Teresa, a humble nun who sacrificed her life in the slums of Calcutta. She did not wait for opportunities; she opened the door. If you have wondered why she was so honored I would suggest it was her....

SIMPLICITY ALONG WITH MERCY

WHEN I heard the host of a Christian television show attempt to interview Mother Teresa I received a new insight into the simplicity of her heart. The interviewer asked her, "Mother, what is love?"

In her unpretentious and quiet manner she simply said, "Love is giving until it hurts, and then continuing to give and give." One could sense that she wanted this interview to be short.

"Mother," he continued, "You must have some goals in life you wish to reach; would you tell us about them?"

She could have bluntly announced, "I do not wish to speak about myself or my goals," yet it was evident that her merciful heart would not expose him or his foolish question. She simply refrained from saying more than, "My only goal is to please Him."

Who was she? As a teenager she felt a calling to full-time church work, and she became a Catholic sister. When she heard a missionary speak of India, she volunteered and was accepted for a teaching post in Calcutta. At the convent in Calcutta, Teresa enjoyed very lovely accommodations that were surrounded by lush gardens.

One day she had to make a trip to the dirtiest part of the town where she saw human beings dying entirely unnoticed. She was so haunted by this terrible situation she felt Jesus Christ was saying to her, "I am calling you to serve the poorest of the poor and to minister not to the living but to the dying."

It took two years, but finally she was released from her vows. No longer a nun, she went out of the convent and into the streets of Calcutta where she prayed, "Jesus, lead me to someone who is dying all alone." Within two blocks she saw an old lady lying in the gutter being eaten by rats. She picked up the woman and literally dragged her to the nearest hospital— where she was refused admittance. She was scolded, "People die in the streets of Calcutta all the time. We cannot take her." She refused to leave until they had taken the dying woman.

Shortly thereafter Teresa went to the city government and asked for an empty room—"a place where I can build a home for the dying." The civil authorities offered her an empty Hindu temple. She announced, "Beautiful! It would be beautiful for God. That is all I want do in my life—something beautiful for God."

Since that time others have joined her as she helped drag the dying from the streets into the temple. She created her own sisterhood called the Sisters of Charity. Amazing blessing flowed from their lives. In due time she was recognized by the Pope who was so impressed when he came to see what this strange ex-nun was doing, that he gave her a gift of his own private, luxurious white limousine. She took one look at this big, expensive car and responded, "Oh! Thank you." Immediately she announced a raffle, sold the car and took the money to her house for the dying. In the years that followed over ten thousand dying lepers passed through her colony. Her colonies spread into twenty-eight cities, to Ceylon, as well as to the Indian people who live in London, Rome, Venezuela and Australia.

When Malcolm Muggeridge interviewed Mother Teresa on the BBC and later visited her in Calcutta he said, "The one thing I noticed about you and the hundreds of sisters who now form your team is that you all look so happy. Is it a put-on?"

She said, "Oh no, not at all. Nothing makes you happier than when you reach out in mercy to someone who is badly hurt."

On another occasion when Mother Teresa attended a meeting in which the nobility from all over the world socialized together, one observer explained, "They were there in their crowns and jewels and silks; Mother wore her plain sari held together by a safety pin." When one of the dignitaries questioned her about her work among the poorest in Calcutta, he asked her if she didn't become discouraged because she saw so little success in her ministry. She was quick to respond, "No, I do not become discouraged. You see God has not called me to a ministry of success. He has called me to a ministry of showing mercy."

PONDER THIS PRINCIPLE: She was available to the lowest, adjustable to unthinkable circumstances and always accountable to the One she loved and sought to please.

MEDITATE ON THIS VERSE: *...the wisdom that comes from heaven is first of all pure, then peace-loving, considerate, submissive, full of mercy and good fruit, impartial and sincere.* (James 3:17 NIV)

WE PRAY: Father, when I look at our Pattern, the Lord Jesus, I am aware of His simplicity of life. How could He as a Man of destiny, who carried the weight of His Father's purpose, remain so simple? I think He would quietly answer, "My only goal is to please Him...and in so doing My priorities are clear."

Daily Focus

_____

_____

_____

_____

_____

_____

_____

After many years of serving the Lord there was fruit evident on his tree—patience, faithfulness, gentleness and self-control were obvious. But there was another character quality yet to be demonstrated when the deacon made…

THE RIGHT BUT DIFFICULT CHOICE

IT IS Sunday morning…Main Street…USA.

Bill has made a choice to attend a Sunday meeting. He has wild hair, wears a T-shirt with holes in it, ragged jeans, and no shoes. But this has been his wardrobe for his entire four years of college.

Bill is brilliant—almost profound in his searching and gentle in his manner. One day Bill makes an encounter on the campus with some awesome kids who help him to a personal relationship with Jesus. Now he knows that he knows this One who has become the Lord of his life. The inward spiritual change in Bill's life is gradually showing outwardly.

Across the street from the campus is a well-dressed, very conservative church. This congregation prays about developing a ministry to the students nearby, but they are not sure just how to go about it.

So, this Sunday morning Bill decides to visit the church he has observed for months. Bill in his unkempt-wild-attire walks into the foyer and then seeks to find a seat. The service has already started, so Bill starts down the middle aisle looking for a spot. Every row is packed and he can't find a seat.

Many people are becoming a bit uncomfortable, but no one says anything or makes any gesture to help Bill. As he walks down the aisle Bill gets closer and closer and closer to the pulpit; suddenly he realizes there are no seats available. So he just squats down right on the carpet in front of the pulpit.

By now, the people are really uptight, and the tension in the air is thick. About this time, the minister realizes that way at the back of the church, a deacon is slowly making his way down the aisle toward Bill. This deacon is in his eighties, has silver-gray hair, and a three-piece suit. Known to be a godly man, he is very elegant, very dignified, very courtly.

The deacon walks with a cane and, as he starts down the aisle walking toward this boy, everyone is thinking that you can't blame him for what he's going to do. After all, how can you expect a man of his age and his background to understand some college kid on the floor in the front of this sanctuary?

It takes some time for the elderly deacon to reach the boy. The church is utterly silent except for the clicking of the man's cane. All eyes are focused on him. The minister stands silently at the pulpit, pauses and waits, for surely he cannot preach his message until the deacon does what he has to do.

Then, they watch as this elderly man drops his cane to the floor. With great difficulty, he lowers himself...and sits down next to Bill so he won't be alone. Everyone chokes with emotion as many reach for their handkerchiefs. When the minister gains control, he announces, "What I'm about to preach, you will not long remember. What you have just seen, you will never forget. Be very careful how you live. You may be the only Bible some people will ever read!"

When the deacon humbly took a place beside Bill, he was embracing an often-missed aspect of the cross: (1) Jesus died on the cross as the substitute for our sins...and we are freely forgiven. (2) But equally as important, we died with Him on the cross...and we can be delivered from our pride and vanity. The deacon was demonstrating this second aspect of the cross—a willingness to embrace "the crucified life."

The Apostle Paul announced, *I have been crucified with Christ and I no longer live, but Christ lives in me. The life I live in this body, I live by faith in the Son of God, who loved me and gave Himself for me.* (Gal. 2:20 NIV)

However hard it is on our pride and our manner of living, let us hear the clear voices of several others who have embraced this same reality of the cross—

– When Dietrich Bonhoeffer, the German minister who died in Nazi hands, explained the focus of his own life, he said, "When God calls a man, He bids him come and die."

– When James Calvert went out as a missionary to the cannibals of the Fiji Islands, the captain of the ship sought to dissuade him. "You will lose your life and the lives of those with you if you go among such savages."

Calvert only replied, "We died before we came here."

– When someone asked George Müller, German pastor, the secret of his victorious life, he replied, "There came a day when George Müller utterly died! No longer did his own desires, preferences, and tastes come first. He knew that from then on Christ must be all in all."

– When Robert Morgan attended college in Columbia, South Carolina, his pastor, Edwin Young, asked him if he knew the secret of Christian victory. He then went on to explain, "You have to put 220 volts to yourself every day." He was, of course, speaking about Gal.2:20, *"I have been crucified with Christ."*

When I read years ago about a sign in the window of a dry-cleaning and dyeing business, I said, "That's the core of our message." The sign stated, "We dye to live, we live to dye; the more we dye, the more we live; and the longer we live, the more we dye."

Now, to keep our doctrine correct we must emphasize that in Christ's death on the cross, we have already died with Him...WE ARE DEAD! It is a finished fact! Yet when Paul again explained that we need to "die daily" he was emphasizing this same choice the elderly deacon made. If someone were to joke that he'd rather die than sit on the floor with ragged Bill then we must all with one voice respond, "Well, die then!"

PONDER THIS PRINCIPLE: The world may mock and scoff at the foolishness of the cross message. But we who know the power of this in our personal experience, know we are as "dead men on furlough!" Yet we are more alive to God and His children than we have ever been.

MEDITATE ON THIS VERSE: *May I never boast except in the cross of our Lord Jesus Christ, through which the world has been crucified to me, and I to the world.* (Gal. 6:14 NIV)

WE PRAY: Father, I want to be available and humble enough when You give me an opportunity to "sit with another" whom the crowd looks down upon.

Daily Focus

_____
_____
_____
_____
_____
_____
_____
_____
_____
_____

The unique privilege of a professor is to teach principles and develop character in students. Sometimes the lessons needing to be learned are challenging and designed to expose weaknesses. To accomplish this end, one professor arranged...

AN UNUSUAL SET-UP

HERE is the true experience of a seminary professor who set up his preaching class one semester. He scheduled each of his students to preach on the Parable of the Good Samaritan. On the day of the class he choreographed his experiment so that each student would go, one at a time, from one classroom to another where he would deliver his sermon.

The professor allowed some students ten minutes to move from one room to another; others were allowed less time, forcing them to rush in order to meet the schedule. Each student, one at a time, had to walk down a certain corridor and pass a hurting bum, who was deliberately planted there, obviously in need of some sort of aid.

The results were surprising, and offered a powerful lesson to them. The percentage of those good men and women who stopped to help was extremely low, especially for those who were under the pressure of a shorter time period. The tighter the schedule, the fewer were those who stopped to help the indigent man.

When the professor revealed his experiment, you can imagine the impact on that class of future spiritual leaders.

Rushing to preach a sermon on the Good Samaritan, they had walked past the "beggar" at the heart of the parable.

Professors do have their goals. Consider another professor who deliberately asked the class in the final question of a quiz, "What is the name of the janitor who works in the halls each day?" Several students raised their hands to ask if that final question would even count. They were disgruntled when he responded, "Absolutely." The professor had deliberately designed it to emphasize character. He explained it was important to personally know and give appreciation to those who diligently serve. He even reminded them that their present reactions to this were also important.

As we consider the Biblical parable, it is possible that Jesus quite deliberately selected the Samaritan, for He had a point to teach. Yes, His story was a set-up.

One morning as I answered the phone, the first words I heard were, "Dr Fromke, are you the one who preaches or the one who practices?"

I realized she was referring to my brother who is a medical doctor, so I tried to "smile over the phone" as I answered, "I would like to believe that both of us practice what we preach." It is my firm conviction that my brother, Vince, really does minister Christ to his patients.

In reading the very first words in the book of Acts we discover this operational principle of our Lord Jesus. It says...of *all that Jesus began both TO DO and TEACH.*

Interesting! Our Lord was always DOING...(first working among them), and from this He was able to explain divine principles (the reason behind His working.)

With this in mind let us seek to get inside of the thinking of each individual, in this story of the Good Samaritan. The priest saw the robbery victim in a half-dead state. Perhaps he felt it was too late for any help to be worthwhile. And according to the Old Testament law, a priest who touched a dead body made himself ceremonially impure (Lev. 21:1-4).

So both the priest and the Levite decided not to get involved. They may even have made a note, "Send out an ambulance." Their professional approach insulates them from being available, and that explains how easy it is to rationalize and pass off the open door of opportunity. Reaching our goal for each day is admirable, yet we need to understand the "as he went" principle, which means we should be sensitive to immediate needs along the way.

Each student in the professor's class faced the intrusion "as he went" to preach his message on the Good Samaritan. So it was necessary to keep focused...and yet adjustable. But how? There is only one way—the inner anointing must constrain one to stop...or to move on. Remember, the inner anointing teaches you all things.

PONDER THIS PRINCIPLE: God has designed our spirit to "sense another dimension beyond human reasoning." Unless we know this difference between our (spirit) intuition and our (mind) reasoning...we cannot walk in the spiritual dimension.

GOD'S WORD: *I will send you the Helper from the Father; He is the Spirit of Truth who comes from the Father. When He comes, He will tell you about Me...* (Jn. 15:26 NCV) Be aware! This Helper is not merely with us but also indwelling us to guide us.

WE PRAY: Father, grant more and more of Your anointing to keep me in step with You...every hour of each day.

Daily Focus

Many divine encounters can seem like tragedies until God turns them into triumphs. In this lesson we will again recognize how He can turn the bitter into sweet. It is only as we move through our immediate pain that we can finally see how He is working to perform...

NOT JUST THE GOOD, BUT THE BEST

IT seemed like the usual Sunday evening service until the pastor approached the pulpit and announced that a very special guest was in attendance. Before giving his evening message, he had invited this visiting minister who was one of his dearest childhood friends to greet the church and share whatever he felt would be appropriate for the service.

An elderly man stepped up to the pulpit and began to share this story: A father, his son and a close friend of his son's were sailing off the Pacific coast one afternoon. Suddenly, without warning, a fast approaching storm blocked any attempt for them to return to the shore. The waves were so high that even though the father was an experienced sailor, he could not keep the boat upright and the three of them were swept into the ocean as the boat capsized.

The elderly speaker hesitated for a moment as he spoke, and made eye contact with two teenagers in the front row of the audience. They began to show keen interest in his story for the first time since he began speaking.

He continued with his story, explaining that as the father grabbed a rescue line, it was suddenly necessary for him to make a most difficult decision. To which boy would he throw the lifeline first? Both boys were struggling in the water. He had only a brief second to decide. The father knew that his own son was an excellent swimmer; he did not know about the swimming skills of his son's friend. He knew that his son was a Christian, but he also realized that his son's friend was not. To whom should he throw the line...that was the agony of this decision he must make.

The father yelled out to his son, "I love you, son!" Then he threw out the lifeline to his son's friend. By the time the father had pulled the friend to the capsized boat, his own son had disappeared beneath the swells of the water into the black deep. His son's body was never recovered.

By this time the two front-row teenagers in the audience were captivated—looking intently for the next words to come out of the elderly minister's mouth.

He continued, "That father rejoiced that his son would step into eternity to be with Jesus...the thought of his son's friend stepping into eternity without Jesus was almost unbearable. As he reflected again on his action, he realized there had been no time to pray or think it through. He had simply reacted on the urge of the moment, when he threw the rescue line to his son's friend, not really aware that it would mean the loss of his own son. But he had made the choice! Was it the right or was it the wrong choice? In a similar manner, this reminds us of our Heavenly Father's willingness to sacrifice His only begotten Son that each of us could be saved. What unfathomable love! Who can explain?"

The elderly minister continued, "There may be someone listening to me right now who needs to reach out and take the lifeline that will rescue him." With those concluding words he turned and sat down in his chair. Silence filled the room. The pastor slowly approached the pulpit and shared a brief message which invited anyone there to personally accept God's lifeline of salvation. The service closed!

Within minutes after the benediction the two teenagers were at the old man's side. "That was a nice story," spoke one of them politely, "but I don't think it was very realistic for that father to give up his own son's life in hopes that the other boy would become a Christian."

"Well, I know you've got a point," the old man replied, glancing down at his worn Bible. Then a big smile broadened his narrow face as he looked into their eyes, "It surely isn't realistic! But I need to emphasize again how that story gives us a deeper insight into what it must have been like for God to give up His lovely Son for us."

Then with a penetrating smile he announced, "You see I was that father who had to make that difficult choice; I was the one who threw out the rescue line. And," he paused briefly, "your pastor was the one I rescued; he was my son's friend. The more I reflect back on that decision, the more I am convinced that God had intervened. It must have been in His plan."

Then the elderly man with tears exhorted them, "Now that you know your pastor was my son's friend, I urge you to carefully listen...HEAR HIM." Two boys stood wiping away their tears and looking with new appreciation at their pastor. From that time on, they determined they would be more attentive to hear what pastor was sharing.

What a divine encounter for those boys and for others in that audience. Out of his great loss the old minister could express tenderness and longsuffering. He was not ministering mere knowledge...but life. It is the most effective way God uses to open eyes. And He did!

PONDER THIS PRINCIPLE: Oswald Chambers said that "the root of all sin is the suspicion that God is not good." So in the middle of shattered dreams, how can I call God good? The answer is simple; we need to recognize that His purpose is not to give us a comfortable life now, but it is to satisfy our soul with Himself...and all that He is.

MEDITATE ON THESE VERSES: *And we know that all things work together for good to those who love God, to those who*

are the called according to His purpose. (Rom. 8:28 NIV)
Wherefore seeing we also are compassed about with so
great a cloud of witnesses, let us lay aside every weight, and
the sin which doth so easily beset us, and let us run with
patience the race that is set before us. (Heb. 12:1 KJV)

WE PRAY: Father, forgive us when we lean upon our own
understanding. We need to heed Your reminder, "Trust Me!
Just trust Me...for all things will work for good to those who
are the called according to My purpose."

Daily Focus

_____
_____
_____
_____
_____
_____
_____
_____
_____
_____
_____
_____
_____
_____

Almost daily we meet Christians who confess, "I keep failing again and again. I wonder—can God still love me? Should I ever expect a deep relationship with Him, when I am so unstable?" A wise counselor has given the hopeful explanation that all of us, in some ways, are failing God. We should never minimize our sins, yet those failures give us, at every moment, new opportunities to...

CELEBRATE HIS GRACE

WHEN a pastor from Pennsylvania visited us, he shared this experience of a lovely woman who attended his church. For more than twenty years she had sought to live an exemplary life among very critical workmates in her office. In spite of her kind and gracious way, she sensed continued hostility to her lifestyle and pondered why there was no apparent fruit from her life.

Then it happened! One morning, in a moment of misunderstanding, she exploded in anger when a false accusation was made. She knew they knew she was innocent, but they refused to acknowledge it. Everyone was surprised, and more amazed! It was unlike her to vent such emotion of anger. She quickly moved from the scene, and remained quiet and isolated for the remainder of the workday.

That evening she explained to her pastor what this terrible episode had done to her Christian testimony. She grieved, "Just think...twenty years of living went down the drain in one brief minute. There is only one thing for me to do. I am convinced I should move to another job."

That wise pastor explained to us how he had counseled her to return to her office in the morning, to call everyone together and, "Ask them to forgive you for your failure and angry response. Do not justify yourself or expose their wrong actions. Simply explain that you failed your Lord...and you are sorry."

She did exactly as he had suggested. Her contrite and humble spirit accomplished what nothing else had done. When she called him that evening, she was jubilant. "They all received my apology!" She explained how one by one "they came to personally assure me they were deeply moved and convicted by their own failure."

The pastor continued his story: "From this I learned that our brokenness seems to be God's way of opening hearts. Each of us is simply an earthen vessel which contains heaven's treasure."

When that sister in brokenness explained her weakness, they saw reality. IT WAS THE BREAK in her earthen vessel that allowed His light to show forth. One of her closest workmates later confided, "Now I know you are real; I recognize this as never before."

When I read God's list of broken things in the Bible, I realize how God uses—for His glory—those people and things that are most completely shattered and broken. In the Old Testament we have several pictures of brokenness:

*Jacob's natural strength had to be broken through a life and death struggle at Peniel before God could clothe him with spiritual power (Gen. 32:22-32).

*When Gideon's 300 soldiers broke their pitchers, light shone forth and struck terror into the hearts of their adversaries (Judg. 7:19-25).

*Mary broke her beautiful alabaster box of ointment and the aroma of lovely perfume filled the house (Matt. 26:6-13).

*When Jesus broke the five barley loaves and two small fish, the food multiplied and became sufficient to feed 5,000 people (John 6:1-14).

*On the cross when Jesus' body was broken by the thorns, the nails, and the spear, redemption poured forth like a crystal stream, cleansing the sinner and giving him life (Matt. 16:26).

If you work in an office or other place of employment, you know what it is like for your associates to observe carefully whether you live up to or fulfill their expectations of a Christian. With God's help you do your best to be "light in a darkened world." Yet you are so very aware that you fall short. But do not forget that even your very humanity...with its Warts, Wrinkles and Weaknesses...is God's way to demonstrate reality. Though critical eyes may be quick to detect some of these three "W"s in you, it is God who will vindicate—when we are willing to be broken—not able, but available!

DON'T EXPECT TO ALWAYS BE APPRECIATED OR UNDERSTOOD BY FRIENDS OR FOES.

Remember in His perfect daily walk our Lord Jesus was misunderstood by the religious zealots of the law. They questioned why he ate with sinners, why He allowed His followers to pluck grain to eat on the Sabbath. Because they misinterpreted Biblical truth, they misunderstood His ways. Don't be surprised if they do the same with you.

It is only human that we shrink back from the pain of being broken. But it is God's way to fruitful service. He stands ready to bear our pain with us, and in due time to mend our broken hearts.

PONDER THIS PRINCIPLE: What is the mark of our Christian life before men? Is it charity? wisdom? sincerity? zeal? Many in the world have these. None of them is peculiar to the people of God, but there is one that is—an amazing absence of self-confidence because God has wrought a deep brokenness in us. Be sure! We do not break ourselves...it is the work of God through brokenness to destroy our self-confidence. He does this in His own time and way.

MEDITATE ON THESE VERSES: *We are the circumcision, who worship by the Spirit of God, and glory in Christ Jesus, and*

PUT NO CONFIDENCE IN THE FLESH. (Phil. 3:3 NIV) For *we which live are always delivered unto death for Jesus' sake, that the life also of Jesus might be made manifest in our mortal flesh.* (2 Cor.4:11 KJV)

WE PRAY: Father, just as our Lord Jesus prayed in the Garden, "Not my will but Thine be done!" So—this is our continual prayer!

Daily Focus

_____
_____
_____
_____
_____
_____
_____
_____
_____
_____
_____
_____
_____
_____
_____
_____
_____
_____

There are untold thousands around us who need acceptance and significance. In today's lesson we consider two teachers with discernment and unique gifting who enabled a student to receive...

THE SIGNIFICANCE NEEDED

IN his daily devotional, David Roper tells about a girl named Mary who was born with a cleft palate. When she started school her classmates teased and taunted her unmercifully because of her scarred and misshapen lips, crooked nose, lopsided teeth, and garbled speech. Mary soon became withdrawn, convinced that no one could love her.

Upon entering second grade, she had a teacher much liked by all the children for her cheerful and affectionate nature. Each year this teacher checked the children's hearing with a simple test. The students would stand across the room from her as she whispered a question such as, "What color are your shoes?" or, "Do you have a new dress?"

When Mary's turn arrived, she listened closely for the teacher's whisper. Then...she heard these extraordinary words: "I wish you were my little girl!"

Wow! Was her teacher really saying and meaning that? Those words changed Mary's life forever. Mary realized she was loved, despite her flawed features, by someone who mattered.

When I read this I was reminded of my growing-up days back in South Dakota where my Aunt Olga taught the second grade in our small town. At the beginning of one school year a fellow teacher explained to my aunt that she had often been distressed by Arlo, a student who was being passed on to my aunt's class. She "wished her much luck" in corralling this young lad. My aunt loved every student, so she willingly accepted the challenge of winning his heart.

Very quickly my aunt was able to diagnose his needs. She invited Arlo to stay after school to help her erase the blackboards, clean erasers—any type of job that needed doing. In a few weeks the whole school became amazed as Arlo's attitude changed. The common comment among teachers walking home together after class was, "Something's happened to Arlo!"

Forty years later when Arlo became one of the prominent leaders in state government, I asked my aunt, "What did you do for Arlo that brought such a change?"

She simply smiled and answered, "I knew he needed some SIGNIFICANCE—so I invited him to be my 'after-school' assistant." In her years as a teacher it was evident she had discernment and a calling to be a "molder" of young lives. She found delight in her ministry!

PONDER THIS PRINCIPLE: Everyone needs a personal identity—WHO they are gives them purpose. But they also need significance—WHAT they are, gives them importance. If this is true in the world around us, it is equally true in God's kingdom. Once we are born into His family, we can say boldly, "Father," because we have a family identity; and when we are fulfilling our special destiny, we become significant both to HIM and to others.

MEDITATE ON THIS VERSE: Paul wrote to his young son-in-the-Lord, Timothy, *[God] hath saved us...and called us...according to his own purpose and grace given us in Christ Jesus before the world began.* (2 Tim. 1: 9 KJV)

WE PRAY: Father, there are "Mary's" and "Arlo's" we know who need special encouragement. Give us eyes to recognize them, and the wisdom to lead them into Your purpose.

Daily Focus

_____

_____

_____

_____

_____

_____

_____

_____

_____

_____

You can allow negativism to reign in your life, or you can choose a life of Divine optimism. Since Adam's fall in the garden most of us have inherited a bent toward seeing the dark side. God's answer is for us to fully embrace the victory of Calvary. When the Apostle Paul exhorted the Philippians to *"think on these things,"* (4:8) he was explaining that the normal Christian life is to accept hindrances and obstacles and make them a door of opportunity. Paul was exhorting us to...

A DIVINE OPTIMISM

I RECENTLY read about a letter from a missionary wife whose husband had been taken by the guerrillas in Sumatra, bound, blindfolded and thrown over a bridge into the river. While he struggled in the water they shot him. His body was never recovered.

Amazingly, some time later his box of belongings was sent to the wife. When she and her son opened the box they discovered the clothes—ruined and worthless. There were also five Bibles in five languages and sermon notes in five languages—priceless mementos. The mother quietly said, "Well, your father didn't leave much, did he?"

Almost instantly the son replied, "But mother, he left a great deal—he witnessed for Christ in five languages. What a privilege!" Then he quietly announced to her, "I'm going

back to Sumatra and take up Dad's work as a missionary."
And he did! He saw the awful curse of darkness, but with
God's grace he turned it into a door of opportunity.

Another story, which I had heard even before I visited
Japan, was about the remarkable life and testimony of
Kagawa—a Japanese Christian whose brutal honesty amazed
and also irritated many. It is significant to know that Kagawa
shared his bed with a beggar and through that contact he
contracted trachoma, the dread eye disease which robbed
him of his sight. But with Divine optimism he answered
them when questioned about his blindness. "Yes," he
reminded them, "but it is inconvenient for people not to have
wings. The reason people create airplanes is to take the place
of wings. The same is true regarding internal eyes. If one
goes blind, it is a matter of creating internal sight...thus God
becomes my light. Even though every outward thing is
shrouded in darkness, in the inner chamber of my soul,
God's eternal light shines."

To those who have sought the secret of Kagawa's poise in
God, he says, "I find no necessity for pessimism. Since I
became God-possessed it has become impossible for me to
commit my soul to wanton thoughts. I glory in the might of
the Almighty who dwells within me." That is Divine optimism!

E.S. Jones writes about a man he met as he came out
from a luncheon at the YMCA. This man of sixty had a bright

smile on his face which captured Jones' attention. When he shook hands with the man, his hands were hard and rough from doing manual labor.

A friend quickly explained, "That man was once a wealthy silk manufacturer. When rayon and nylon were invented his silk business was ruined and he was reduced to zero. But he has met the loss with simple joy. One of his greatest pleasures now is to go and play on the organ of a church to which he contributed $25,000 in the days of his wealth." But most importantly, he is victorious! This loss of his business became a door of opportunity which led him into Divine optimism. Since he is now able to be thankful for the worst that happened, he cannot be tormented by other fears of loss.

Please know that we are not endorsing "self-improvement" which emphasizes the message of "You can do better; you can be happier." In most cases that is a formula mentality—a formula that promises if you will do this, then that will happen. The self-help books focus on improvement and self-satisfaction, but God's way is brokenness into peace.

Larry Crabb, counselor, warns, "I don't think (self-satisfaction) is the direction of Scriptures at all. I think God's word has much more to do with whether I am more deeply a pleasure to God. Yes, I struggle with the self-help movement (because) I don't think it involves the brokenness that is required to reach the goal God has for us."

PONDER THIS PRINCIPLE: If we really understand Divine Optimism we recognize it is not a reformation of our attitudes; rather it is a resurrection. Out of our brokenness and death is emerging a whole new life perspective which, I must warn you, is very contagious to those with whom it comes in contact. Yes, BROKENNESS BRINGS BLESSING.

MEDITATE ON THESE VERSES: The Apostle Paul exhorts us, *Let this mind be in you, which was also in Christ Jesus.* (Phil.2:5 KJV) and *Finally...whatsoever things are true...honest...just...pure...lovely...think on these things.* (Phil. 4:8 KJV)

WE PRAY: Father, I ask for clarity in my own mental outlook, and also for some of my friends who need to be released from continually seeing the "dark side of life." I thank You that this choice can become an attitude and a way of life.

Daily Focus

Everything in this book can be nullified if you become a victim of one of today's most pervasive problems—the spirit of depression and discouragement. As long as your spirit is strong and confident you can face up to anything. But if you let your spirit become crushed you have no resisting power. Consider God's plan for...

CURING YOUR DEPRESSION

HEAR this testimony of a man who had hit bottom. Everything crashed in on him—his wife had left him, he lost his job, and he was utterly discouraged, completely depressed. It seemed so bad he lost faith in other people, lost self-esteem and even began to blame God.

Early one bleak, rainy morning, this man went into a diner for breakfast. Several people were there, but no one was speaking to anyone else—and our friend hunched disconsolately on a stool. At the other end of the diner a young mother and a little girl had been seated at the counter. When their plate of food was set down, suddenly the little girl's voice broke the silence. "Don't we say grace here, Mommy?"

Behind the counter, the big, surly cook looked at the little girl and growled, "Sure we do, honey. Will you say it for us?" And he glared at everyone present, "Bow your heads!"

One by one heads went down. The little girl bowed her head, clasped her hands and said,

"God is great and God is good
  And we thank Him for our food.
By His hand we all are fed;
  Give us Lord, our daily bread.
In Jesus' name, Amen."

All of a sudden the atmosphere in the diner changed. The people present began talking to each other, and the plain old diner unexpectedly turned into a home, all because a little girl gave thanks to God for her food.

"All of a sudden," explained our discouraged friend, "my heart seemed to open up and a light came into my mind; a Bible verse came to remembrance. I later discovered it was Isaiah 41:10, *Fear thou not, for I am with thee: be not dismayed; for I am thy God: I will strengthen thee, yea, I will help thee...* (KJV)

From that diner experience my life outlook changed. I no longer accepted the lie of the enemy that God was against me. When I realized just how much He loved me, the depression left and I began to give thanks for the unspeakable mercy of God.

PONDER THIS PRINCIPLE: I am continually reminding folk that in the Bible God has written 365 times...(one for each day of the year)... *"Fear not..."*

MEDITATE ON THESE VERSES: *I sought the Lord, and He heard me, and delivered me from all my fears.* (Psa. 34:4 KJV)

The eyes of the Lord are upon the righteous, and His ears are open to their cry. (Psa. 34:15 KJV)

WE PRAY: Father, like that little girl, I want to honor You in every situation. Who knows how a bit of Your Life and Light may change the atmosphere around me. You are the Great Changer!

Daily Focus

_____

_____

_____

_____

_____

_____

_____

_____

_____

_____

_____

_____

_____

_____

_____

_____

OPPORTUNITY for prayer presents itself, but we must recognize the door. Here is a great way to redeem the minutes if you find waiting difficult. Consider how Louise learned to

MEET THE NEEDS OF OTHERS

I WAITED for my husband a long time in the car in the parking lot. It was a hot day and I had finished the book I was reading. I was beginning to feel bored and frustrated. "What an opportunity to pray," I thought. "I'm alone and I have a lot of things to pray about. I'm concerned about my family, my health, my finances...my...!"

I closed my eyes and tried to pray, but I couldn't concentrate. Every movement around the car took my attention. I became irritated with myself—that a mature person couldn't keep focused...!

Then as I opened my eyes I saw an elderly woman walking slowly with one hand on her hip. "It hurts," I thought, and I found my heart reaching out in prayer for her...her pain, her need for others to come along side.

"Now I can get back to praying about my concerns," I thought, but suddenly my attention was drawn to the cry of a baby. I looked around for the baby and saw a young mother, much too small to be carrying such a big baby. The child was struggling, wanting to get down, and I could see her talking softly to him. She looked tired and harried—so I began to pray for her. I asked God to give her the strength and patience and the joy of motherhood.

Then I saw two elderly gentlemen walking together in animated conversation—brothers? friends? I prayed that God would make any adjustment they seemed to need.

A well-dressed man, jauntily swinging a briefcase, hurried through my field of vision—but not before I prayed for him to make time for God in his busy day.

Right in my line of sight was a young woman helping an elderly woman from the car. Her whole demeanor was one of love and care. I asked God to bless her and make their time together a blessing.

Stumbling slightly, an unkempt young man made his way between the cars. He needed a shave and some clean clothes—so I held him up before the Lord—asking God to meet his deepest needs.

Then it seemed lots of people were coming and going in the parking lot. I couldn't focus long on them, but asked God to single out those who needed help most. Suddenly I realized I wasn't bored anymore—I was excited!

Next a young couple, hand in hand, walked past—talking seriously together, obviously in love. I prayed that they would allow God to become the central focus of their lives—instead of seeking to find happiness in each other.

Two teenaged boys ran through the lot and out into the traffic, so I asked God to keep them safe and diligent in their school work.

What a parade of people to pray for...and I suddenly realized I had no problem focusing on prayer for those around me. And more importantly, I had forgotten myself, my problems, and my concerns. My thoughts and the time flew by—so much time that I was almost disappointed when my husband returned.

As we were pulling out of the lot, I saw a husband and wife arguing, so I prayed quickly for God to bring resolution—not just immediate peace, but to disclose the deeper issues that would hinder lasting harmony.

PONDER THIS PRINCIPLE: It is possible to ask God for a temporary FIX, in times of need, but we must help our eyes to discern the root issues.

MEDITATE ON THIS VERSE: It is likely the Apostle Paul understood what Louise was discovering when he wrote, *Pray without ceasing.* (1 Thess. 5:17 KJV) Was that really possible for anyone?

Even in that time when life surely moved at a much slower pace, Paul recognized the propensity for getting caught in the busyness...the pressures of meeting schedules, and the desperate cries of needy people.

WE PRAY: Father, I begin to realize it is possible for my heart to keep tuned...to You, so I can be attuned to the needs of others.

Daily Focus

_____

_____

_____

_____

_____

_____

_____

_____

_____

_____

_____

_____

_____

_____

_____

_____

_____

_____

_____

_____

_____

All of us enjoy reading how God led His people Israel, from Egypt through the wilderness to Canaan. But we have pondered why a loving God would put His people through such severe testing. Did God mean this to be an opportunity—a schoolroom—for learning to know more about Him? Yes, but they failed in the most critical lesson of hearing His voice daily. As a consequence they began...

USING YESTERDAY'S DIRECTIONS

ONLY those who have spent time in a hot desert wilderness can appreciate one's imperative need for water. Can you imagine how much water a million or more Israelites would need each day just to survive?

We read (Exodus 15) that Israel went three days into the wilderness of Shur and found no water. We encounter the first of their murmurings, "What shall we drink?" Be patient with their leader, Moses, who cried unto the Lord. He was shown a tree, which he cast into the bitter water and it became sweet.

We must remember! Israel is just three days into their journey! Is this a consequence of some disobedience, or is it a conflict allowed by God to prove them? I am convinced this was an opportunity arranged by God. While they did not realize it, they were just entering God's schoolroom.

So, God presents to them the governing principle of their entire journey. *...If thou wilt diligently hearken to the voice of the Lord thy God and wilt do...* (Exodus 15:26) How simple! How important! Just "listen and do." All the lessons in their schoolroom journey (and ours) with God will center in this one issue "today, if you will listen..." HOW WONDERFUL! They were to have the privilege of daily receiving special instructions for each new step of the way.

Three months pass; now they come to another "no water" situation. Once again they murmur, "Give us water to drink." So Moses seeks the face of the Lord and is given new direction to "stand before the people and smite the rock"...and watch water come forth.

We can all identify in some way with these Israelites. At one time or another I'm sure you have faced a "no water" situation. You have no money, no job, no food, no place to live, and no one understands your predicament. You wrestle with your dilemma and question why this has happened! Have you missed God's will? How could this happen to you, who belong to the Lord? How could this be in God's leading? At this point, the enemy is quick to whisper that you've really missed God's will and this is a consequence. Yet God will explain, "This is a conflict in which you will have opportunity to really know Me and My ways more fully."

It is so important to understand that all the trials of God's people are intended to be educatory...not punitive! Yes—you can enjoy your lessons in God's school or you can murmur and resist the teacher.

Remember God's primary lesson to the Israelites, "today, if you will listen..." Please note—during the first trial Moses placed a tree in the bitter water; in this second trial when they need water Moses strikes a rock. And we hasten ahead (much later) to their third "no water" experience when the Lord tells Moses to "speak to the rock!" We marvel at this progressive unfolding! God has new directions for each crisis. Why? It's because He wants us to understand the unique privilege of daily "hearing His voice" for new directions.

Someone is about to ask, "What is the value in getting new directions if we can't use them again?" Oh, if we are only concerned for ourselves, there is none; but if we want to help others.... Yes! Let us review a bit. Moses cut a tree to turn the bitter water into sweet water, next he struck the rock, and then he spoke to the rock. We might ponder what new direction might have come next. We do not know. But the lesson is clear; it is always better to have THE GUIDE than to have His guidance.

PONDER THIS PRINCIPLE: We can be the object of His blessing, or we can choose to become a channel. What experience we gain is not just for ourselves, but also for others. In seeking to help others, we can explain from our own experience how God has turned our bitter situations into sweet, as we view them through

>...the perspective of the cross...a tree cut down;
>...the striking of the cross...Christ crucified;
>...the speaking to the Rock...Christ resurrected.

It is noteworthy: the Hebrew word for that second rock means a "high lifted up" rock. Christ was crucified once, now we are to be occupied with our resurrected Lord who is daily interceding for us.

It was an unusual privilege for Israel to know their God, and to marvel in His ways. No other nation (before or since) has ever been granted such unique opportunity. As we observe their entire forty year journey, we are ashamed to report their ten murmurings (complaints) because they could not appreciate the purpose of their testings.

MEDITATE ON THESE VERSES: Consider how God exhorts us as New Testament believers, *Now all these things happened unto them for an example: and they are written for our admonition upon whom the ends of the age is come. Therefore let him who thinks he stands take heed lest he fall.* (1 Cor. 10:11-12 NKJV)

WE PRAY: Father, we do not want to be part of that murmuring crowd. We will heed the Apostle Paul's exhortation, *God is faithful! He will not allow us to be tested beyond what we are able but will with the testing make a way of escape that you may be able to bear it.* (1 Cor. 10:13)

Daily Focus

_____

_____

_____

_____

_____

_____

_____

_____

_____

_____

_____

_____

_____

_____

_____

_____

_____

_____

_____

_____

_____

_____

IN FACING AN IMPOSSIBLE TASK, He gave this word: *...I have set before you an open door, and no one can shut it:, for you have a little strength, have kept My word, and have not denied My name.* (Rev. 3:8 NKJV) The impossible task then became a...

DOOR OF OPPORTUNITY

CONSIDER this story of an elderly missionary couple who had been working in Africa for many years and were returning to New York City to retire. With no pension and broken health, they were discouraged and even fearful of the future.

They happened to be booked on the same ship as Teddy Roosevelt, who was returning from a big-game hunting expedition. They watched the passengers trying to glimpse the great man and the crew fussing over him. At the dock in New York there was even a band waiting to greet the President. But the missionary couple slipped off the ship unnoticed.

That night, in a cheap flat they found on the East Side, the man's spirit broke. He said to his wife, "I can't take this; God is not treating us fairly! Why was no one there to meet us? We are faced with the impossible—returning home unknown, uncared for and with an uncertain future."

His wife suggested he go into the bedroom and tell the Lord. A short time later he came out with a completely different countenance. His wife asked, "Dear, what happened?"

"The Lord settled it with me," he said. "I told Him how impossible our situation seemed and even how bitter I felt that the President should receive this tremendous homecoming, when no one met us as we returned home. And when I finished, it seemed as though the Lord put his hand on my shoulder and simply said, 'But you're not home yet!'"

Many years ago when I first read this account, it suddenly brought to mind this old spiritual:

"This world is not my home; I'm just a passing thru.

My treasures are laid up, somewhere beyond the blue."

We do not know what happened to this missionary couple! But we feel sure they really didn't retire, they simply refired. Because we are not called to a place but rather to a purpose, we are sure they continued through the next "door of opportunity" which the Lord set before them.

...I have set before you an open door!... (Rev. 3:8) This verse has become a personal benchmark several times as I have faced a door of opportunity, especially one that seemed far beyond my capabilities. This promise has become a SURE FOUNDATION STONE that has under-girded me.

The word "opportunity" in its root meaning is "the open door." So you become convinced that as you walk with Jesus everything is an opportunity—virtually an open door. When you are in Him, then anything that ever happens to you can be turned into an open door. If the worst happens—sin, and sin is the very worst thing that can happen to you—then even that becomes an open door, for it drives you to the Redeemer.

But you say, I do not feel so sinful as I feel empty. Even your emptiness is an opportunity in Jesus. Yes, "there is the emptiness of the reed through which the musician makes music; the emptiness of the womb in which a child will be nourished; the emptiness of the cup to be filled with the wine of His Presence" (ESJ). In Jesus everything is an opportunity.

PONDER THIS PRINCIPLE: It is such a blessing to know that all our treasures are measured by Him in the light of eternity, and since we only live to please Him, we can rejoice. Though we may have missed some opportunities, He is a loving Father who loves us anyway. If He is satisfied with us, then we can be satisfied.

GOD'S WORD: The apostle Paul was very much aware that it was God who would open doors:

...Praying...that God would grant unto us a door of utterance, to speak the mystery of Christ, for which I am also in bonds. (Col. 4:3 KJV)

...A great door and effectual is opened unto me, and there are many adversaries. (1 Cor. 16:9 KJV)

...When I came to Troas...a door was opened unto me of the Lord. (2 Cor. 2:12 KJV)

WE PRAY: *Now thanks be unto God, which always causes us to triumph in Christ, and maketh manifest the savour of His knowledge by us in every place.* (2 Cor. 2:14 KJV)

Daily Focus

_____

_____

_____

_____

_____

_____

_____

_____

_____

_____

_____

_____

_____

_____

_____

_____

_____

_____

_____

_____

_____

Each of us can look back with regret on some opportunity we could have used for God's glory. Robert Peterson explains an incident that changed his life forever. May it serve as a reminder to all of us. We need to take time to enjoy living and loving each other. Knowing God intimately means getting quiet. Life is so complicated; the hustle and bustle of everyday traumas can cause us to lose our focus on…

WHAT IS REALLY IMPORTANT

SHE was six years old when I first met her on the beach near where I live. I drive to this beach whenever the world begins to close in on me. She was building a sandcastle or something, and looked up, her eyes as blue as the sea. "Hello," she said.

I answered with a nod, not really in the mood to bother with a small child.

"I'm building," she said.

"I see that. What is it?" I asked not really caring.

"Oh, I don't know. I just like to feel the sand."

"That sounds good," I thought, and slipped off my shoes. A sandpiper glided by.

"That's a joy," the child said.

"It's what?"

"It's a joy. My mama says sandpipers come to bring us joy."

The bird went gliding down the beach. "Goodbye joy," I muttered to myself, "hello pain," and turned to walk on. I was depressed; my life seemed completely out of balance.

"What's your name?" She wouldn't give up.

"Robert," I answered. "I'm Robert Peterson."

"Mine's Wendy...I'm six."

"Hi, Wendy."

She giggled. "You're funny," she said.

In spite of my gloom, I laughed too and walked on. Her musical giggle followed me.

"Come again, Mr. P," she called. "We'll have another happy day."

After a few days with a group of Boy Scouts, PTA meetings, and an ailing mother, the sun was shining one morning as I took my hands out of the dishwater. "I need a sandpiper," I said to myself, gathering up my coat. As I arrived, the ever-changing balm of the seashore awaited me. The breeze was chilly but I moved along, trying to capture the serenity I needed.

"Hello, Mr. P," Wendy called out. "Do you want to play?

"What did you have in mind?" I asked sarcastically.

The twinkling laughter burst forth again. "I don't know..."

"Then let's just walk." Looking at her, I noticed the delicate fairness of her face.

"Where do you live?" I asked.

"Over there." She pointed toward a row of summer cottages.

Strange, I thought, in winter. "Where do you go to school?

"I don't go to school. Mommy says we're on vacation."

She chattered little-girl talk as we strolled up the beach, but my mind was on other things. When I left for home, Wendy said it had been a happy day. Feeling surprisingly better, I smiled at her and agreed.

Three weeks later, I rushed to the beach in a state of near panic. I was in no mood to even greet Wendy. I thought I saw her mother on the porch and felt like demanding she keep her child at home.

"Look, if you don't mind," I said crossly when Wendy caught up with me, "I'd rather be alone today." She seemed unusually pale and out of breath.

"Why?" she asked.

I turned to her and shouted, "Because my mother died!" and then I thought...My God, why was I saying this to a little child?"

"Oh," she said quietly, "then this is a bad day."

"Yes," I said, "and yesterday and the day before and—oh go away!"

"Did it hurt?" she inquired.

"Did what hurt?" I was exasperated with her...with myself.

"When she died?

"Of course it hurt!" I snapped, misunderstanding. Wrapped up in myself, I strode off.

A month or so later, when I went to the beach she wasn't there. Feeling guilty, ashamed and admitting to myself that I missed her, I went up to the cottage after my walk and knocked at the door. A drawn looking young woman with honey-colored hair opened the door.

"Hello," I said, "I'm Robert Peterson. I missed your little girl today and wondered where she was."

"Oh, yes, Mr. Peterson, please come in. Wendy spoke of you so much. I'm afraid I allowed her to bother you. If she was a nuisance, please accept my apologies."

"Not at all—she's a delightful child," I said, suddenly realizing that I meant what I had just said.

"Wendy died last week, Mr. Peterson. She had leukemia. Maybe she didn't tell you."

Struck dumb, I groped for a chair. I had to catch my breath.

"She loved this beach, so when she asked to come, we couldn't say no. She seemed so much better here and had a lot of what she called happy days. But the last weeks she declined rapidly..." her voice faltered. "She left something for you...if only I can find it. Could you wait a moment while I look?"

I nodded stupidly, my mind racing for something to say to this lovely young mother. She handed me a smeared envelope with "Mr. P" printed in gold childish letters. Inside was a drawing in bright crayon hues—a yellow beach, a blue sea, and a brown bird. Underneath was carefully printed: A SANDPIPER TO BRING YOU JOY.

Tears welled up in my eyes and a heart that had almost forgotten how to love opened wide. I took Wendy's mother in my arms. "I'm sorry, I'm so sorry," I muttered over and over, and we wept together.

The precious little picture is framed now and hangs in my study. Six words—one for each year of her life—that speak of harmony, courage, and undemanding love. It's a gift from a child with sea-blue eyes and hair the color of sand, who opened the door for me to know Him more intimately.

PONDER THIS PRINCIPLE: God can mend your broken heart, but you must give Him all the pieces. So often we reserve some hidden section of our heart. And we can rejoice in this: God loves His children not because of who they are, but because of WHO HE IS. We are loved with unconditional love...His love.

MEDITATE ON THIS VERSE: *Beloved, let us love one another, for love is of God; and everyone who loves is born of God and knows God.* (1 John 4:7 NKJV)

WE PRAY: Father, I ask that You will help us to take time to fellowship with "the little folk" who often seem like a nuisance. We close these lessons, but we will continue to wait for You to open doors of OPPORTUNITY.

Daily Focus

_____

_____

_____

_____

_____

_____

_____

_____

_____

_____

_____

_____

_____

_____

_____

_____

_____

_____

FROM OUR PARTNERS

ONE DAY we received the following story in a letter:

Some friends explained how they had left home to attend a wedding in a distant state, leaving their dog in the care of their neighbor, as usual. The first day when he entered the house he observed a book on the coffee table where he usually sat while watching the dog eat. He picked up the book and the first story caught his attention, so he took the book home with him. He pondered…just maybe these neighbors intended for him to read this book placed there on the table. Anyway the book became the center of attention as he, along with his wife, read every story—and enjoyed the "fifteen day journey."

Upon the friends' return, the neighbor and his wife came to welcome them back home announcing, "We are ready! We have a desire to become Christians. That book you left on the table for us to read has shown us our need for Christ. Please help us; we know you have been praying." (At the end of each daily story there was a place for prayer requests…and answers.)

Of course it was a joyous time to discover how God had arranged this appointment. Now the friends were writing to explain why they were buying cartons of books to share. We bowed to thank God—for His own way of creating Doors of Opportunity.

BEFORE WE LEAVE....

YOU MAY SHARE A FOCUS

THIS is your opportunity to purchase these stories to share with friends or your study group. Our dedication is to make these available in carton quantities at a very low price.

DO NOT JUST OFFER A GIFT. We encourage you to wisely open to some "lesson" in this manual, which may be exactly the help or the answer to meet a need. Recently I read a portion of a story to the office manager in our complex. When I had his interest I left the stories with him. He got so interested he quickly finished reading all the lessons. (And now many others have become interested.)

It has been our discovery that most folk will politely accept a gift—and it moves from your bookshelf to theirs unread. It is important to create enough interest to get their attention.

REMEMBER you are in real competition for people's time. Everyone is so preoccupied with THEIR IMMEDIATE CONCERNS they will hardly take time to FOCUS ON THEIR DEEPER NEEDS.

God has HIS TIMING for every situation. Today you may plant and pray. Then you can wait to water the seed and pray for God's open door of opportunity to present the claims of Christ in each life.

TODAY YOU CAN BECOME A PARTNER IN A GROWING COMPANY OF OPPORTUNISTS...

who seek to be discerning, diligent and devoted.

I am grateful for their help:

...to Steve Cannon for designing the covers,
...to DeVon for servicing our computers,
...to Michele Captain: I have always wanted a daughter. Now the Lord has given one who is diligent and devoted and discerning.
...my wife, Ruth—who is God's Gracious Gift to me. Always helpful—discerning exactly what needs to be done.
...I give my thanks...but even more importantly:
  THE LORD IS PLEASED WITH YOUR LABOR.

OTHER BOOKS BY DEVERN FROMKE

Life's Ultimate Privilege

This fifteen day journey has become a favorite. Many churches
and study groups have used these lessons to stimulate personal
and corporate growth. Now over 210,000 copies in a short time
demonstrate both the challenge and value of this devotional book.

The Larger Window

This selection of 100 amazing stories will demonstrate how God
can move each of us from being objects of grace, mercy and
peace to BECOME channels and models to bless others. While
the stories are both entertaining and challenging, the author has
one definite goal: to move each of us from our preoccupation with
what we can get from God to what He will get as we become
wholly alive unto Him for fulfilling His purpose.

The Ultimate Intention

This classic has been revised with a study guide for those who
desire class participation. For more than 40 years DeVern
Fromke's writings have emphasized the God-centered view of
reality as imperative for our vision and growth. It is no
exaggeration to say that this volume has radically altered the
ministry of many key leaders in this country and around the world.
Now over 200,000 copies and in many languages, this volume will
move every reader from a self-center to God-centeredness.

Unto Full Stature

This newly revised volume unveils very practical outworking of the
Ultimate truth. The author attempts to lead each one step by step
through eight levels or phases of our natural and spiritual maturity.
He exposes hidden reasons why the child of God flounders in
spiritual perspective, often disregards the place of the will and too
often abuses his body as he zealously lives at exhaustion point.
Many churches have used this with classroom participation.